Fact Finders®

See It,
Write It

Picture Yourself
writing
DRAMA

Using **Photos** to
Inspire Writing

by Barbara A. Tyler

CAPSTONE PRESS
a capstone imprint

Fact Finders are published by Capstone Press,
151 Good Counsel Drive, P.O. Box 669, Mankato, Minnesota 56002.
www.capstonepub.com

Books published by Capstone Press are manufactured with paper
containing at least 10 percent post-consumer waste.

Library of Congress Cataloging-in-Publication Data
Tyler, Barbara A.
 Picture yourself writing drama : using photos to inspire writing / by Barbara A. Tyler.
 p. cm.—(Fact finders. see it, write it)
 Includes bibliographical references and index.
 Summary: "Useful tips and writing prompts show young writers how to use images to inspire drama
writing"—Provided by publisher.
 ISBN 978-1-4296-6126-3 (library binding)
 ISBN 978-1-4296-7203-0 (paperback)
 1. Playwriting—Juvenile literature. 2. Literature and photography—Juvenile literature. I. Title.
PN1661.T95 2012
808.2—dc22   2010052358

Editorial Credits
Jennifer Besel, editor; Veronica Correia, designer; Eric Manske, production specialist

Photo Credits
Alamy: Tim Graham, 16; Corel, 11, 12, 17, 23; Dreamstime: Dundanim, 19, Raulsm, 25; EyeWire,
20; Getty Images Inc.: The Image Bank/Steven Puetzer, 6; Image courtesy of Click Portrait Studio, 32;
iStockphoto: Duncan Walker, 18, Uygar Ozel, 9; NASA, 27; Shutterstock: Bobby Deal/RealDealPhoto,
3, 8, Fedor Selivanov, 10, Knud Nielsen, 22, Lane V. Erickson, 24, Lexy Sinnott, 29, Luciano Mortula,
cover, marilyn barbone, 1, 13, markh, 7, MaxFX, 14, Neil Roy Johnson, 26, Peter Kirillov, 15, Sari
ONeal, 5, Yuri Arcurs, 21

Printed in the United States of America in Stevens Point, Wisconsin.
032011   006111WZF11

TABLE OF CONTENTS

Acting on Ideas

Have you ever been wrapped up in the action of a good movie?

Your heart pounds as you clutch your popcorn. You perch on the edge of your seat, wondering what will happen next.

Maybe you've had this reaction to a play or TV show. Each of these **mediums** start out as pieces of writing called dramas. A drama, also called a script, is meant to be acted out.

Writing a drama calls for a lot of imagination. How will the stage look? What will the characters say? What problems will they face? Your choices will bring a story to life.

But what if your ideas have stage fright, and your words are hiding backstage? Instead of staring at a blank page, look at a photograph. A photo can inspire an idea for a story, a character, or a plot. The following tips and exercises will show you how to uncover ideas hiding in photographs. All you have to do is pounce on them.

> **medium**—something that communicates messages, such as TV, movies, and the Internet

The  Writing Process

Step 1 Prewrite

Plan what you're going to write. Are you going to write a drama, a poem, or some other form of writing? Choose a topic, and start brainstorming details. Also identify your audience and the purpose of your piece.

Step 2 Draft

Put your ideas on paper. Start crafting your composition. Don't worry about getting the punctuation and grammar perfect. Just start writing.

Step 3 Revise

Check your work for ways to improve your writing. Fix areas that are confusing. Look for spots that need reorganizing. Are there places where you could make the words more clear or exciting? Having other people look at your work might be helpful too.

Step 4 Edit

Now look for those pesky punctuation errors. Also check your spelling, grammar, and capitalization.

Step 5 Publish

When you're done, share your work! You can present it to a class or post it online. Maybe you could have it printed in your school newspaper. The possibilities for sharing your work are endless.

Chapter 1

SET IT UP

story ideas

All dramas begin with a story idea. Finding one is a snap with a great photo. All you have to do is think like a reporter. Ask yourself the who, what, where, when, why, and how questions. Dreaming up the answers will give you a story idea.

This picture might make you ask:

· When did it happen? *during an important dinner*

· Why is it important? *If the dinner doesn't go well, the restaurant will close.*

· What happened? *a microwave meltdown*

· Who was involved? *a chef*

· Where did it happen? *a struggling restaurant*

· How does everything turn out? *After the restaurant closes, the chef turns the microwave into a piece of art. The doomed restaurant becomes a famous art museum.*

It's OK if the picture makes you think of something totally different than what you see. This small mess might make you think of something bigger ... like an explosion!

The whole idea behind using photos is to get your imagination going.

write about It!

What does this photo make you think of? Ask yourself who, what, where, when, why, and how. As you brainstorm, write down your questions and their answers. Invent more than one answer for each question. Be creative. What kinds of twists can you dream up? When you're done, choose your favorite answers. Then write a few sentences describing your story idea.

Plot

Before you sit down to write, make a story map. Whether you're writing a **skit** or a three-act play, a map helps you navigate through the plot in your script.

Making a story map is as simple as writing a list. Start with the overall problem. What is the character trying to do? Then add problems that grow tougher for the character to solve. Finally, end with the resolution.

Need help getting started?

Photos can spark action ideas for your plot. This photo might suggest a story about a boxing tournament. Start your map by creating a conflict.

Conflict: Ally needs prize money from a boxing tournament to pay for college.

Next, add what happens as Ally works toward her goal.

1. She trains every day with a trainer who secretly wants her to lose.

2. During a practice, her trainer trips her. Ally gets hurt and has to drop out of the tournament.

3. Ally helps her friend train for the tournament.

Resolution: Thanks to Ally, her friend wins the tournament. A boxing school learns about Ally's skill. They offer her a job that will help pay for school.

write about It!

Who is wearing these boots? What's the problem? What steps will he or she take to solve it? What will get in the way? Use your ideas to map out a plot. First, write down the problem. Then list each action that happens as the character tries to solve the problem. Finally, tell how everything turns out. Now you've got a map to follow. Use it to create a short skit.

skit—a short play

Setting

Every story takes place somewhere. Where does your drama happen? A cool photo can help you travel to a unique **setting**.

The setting for each **scene** in a drama is described in a scene description.

Where does the story take place?

What props belong on the stage?

Are there other people in the scene besides the main characters?

The scene description answers those questions using powerful details. Strong descriptions guarantee that people putting on your drama will know exactly how the stage should look.

Let a photo transport your mind to a setting. Then describe what you see. Be specific.

What are these stairs made of? Concrete or marble? Both words are more exact than saying "stone."

Are the people loud or quiet?

Include as many details as you can in your drama's scene descriptions.

SCENE: Troy and Mike nervously wait in the museum lobby. A whispering crowd is gathered around an enormous, marble staircase.

setting—the place where a drama takes place

scene—a part of a story that shows what is happening in one place and time

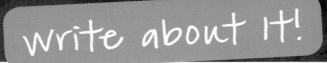

write about It!

Ready for a trip? Let this photo be your passport to a setting for your drama. Where will it take you? Brainstorm strong adjectives and nouns that will paint a picture of what you imagine. Then weave those words into a description for the opening scene of a drama.

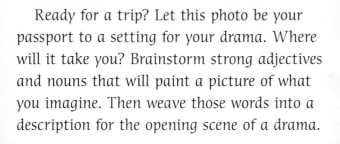

Chapter 2

WHO DID IT?

Main character

The main character is the most important person in a drama. He or she has problems to solve and a story to tell. That's a big job for one person. To fill the role, you'll need a character full of personality. Great pictures can help.

Look at this fellow. His personality should be as colorful as his face. Use a character profile to get to know him. A character profile is a collection of facts about the character. Where does he come from? What does he do? What are his problems, secrets, and goals? If you create lots of unusual details, you'll have a main character who stands out.

This photo might inspire a character profile with facts like these.

TOPIC	FACT
Name	Kofi (means born on Friday)
Age	20
Home	small apartment in Boston, Massachusetts
Family life	has two brothers; lives with dad and grandma
History	Mom left when he was little.
Job	works with brothers as a street dancer in a park
Goal or problem	wants to earn enough money to hire a detective to find his mother

write about It!

Imagine a character profile based on the person in this picture. What is her life like? What are her hopes and dreams? What makes her different from other characters? Think of 10 things that make her an individual, and put them in a character profile. Then use the profile to write a monologue that introduces the character to the audience.

monologue—a long speech by one character

Sidekicks and Villains

The main character isn't the only person in a drama. He or she needs sidekicks to help and villains to cause trouble.

That's a bunch of characters. But don't worry. With photos, dreaming up more characters is as easy as 1-2-3!

1. CHOOSE A COOL PHOTO FOR YOUR CHARACTER.

2. CREATE A CHARACTER PROFILE.

3. USE THE PROFILE TO WRITE A CHARACTER SKETCH.

A character sketch is a written piece that tells the **backstory** of a character. The sketch helps answer why the character acts a certain way.

Here's a brief profile for this image.

Name	Aisha
Talent	can hypnotize people
Likes	mysteries and surprises
Dislikes	injustice

Then in the character sketch, answer why she hates injustice or why she likes mysteries. To make all your characters stand out, create a profile and a sketch for each one. Use the details you create to fill your drama with powerful, deep characters.

A long time ago, Aisha was kicked off a bus for something she didn't do. Later, she learned to hypnotize people. She returned to the bus and hypnotized the driver, making him very kind. Aisha's secret pleasure became fighting injustice without anyone knowing it was her.

backstory—a story that tells what happened before the main story

write about It!

Check out this crazy-looking dog. Imagine it belongs to the villain of your drama. Create a character profile for this villain. Then use the profile to write a character sketch. Describe three ways the villain and his or her pet caused trouble in the past. Don't forget to include why the villain acts evil.

Chapter 3

TELLING THE STORY

Dialogue

Talk, talk, talk. That's the way you tell the story in a drama.

Dialogue needs to move the plot forward, set the scene, and introduce the audience to the characters. If your characters are tongue-tied, a photo can help you put words in their mouths. This image might remind you of a prank. What will the characters say about it? Explore your ideas by writing a story idea in paragraph form first.

Sam and Ann spotted the sculpture on Mr. Brown's roof. They didn't believe the local bad-boy Charlie had done it. But they knew he would get the blame.

Next, transform your paragraph into dialogue. Let the characters share the information with the audience.

SAM: *I don't believe it! Look! Mr. Brown's sculpture is on his roof!*

ANN: *Do you think Charlie did it? He did just get out of jail.*

SAM: *Nah, but he's gonna get blamed.*

Keep it real. Good dialogue sounds like a real conversation. To hear how your dialogue sounds, take it for a test drive. Read it aloud, and revise any parts that sound odd or clunky.

write about It!

Imagine that these two characters are on vacation together. Write dialogue for a conversation between them. Think of things they could say to describe the setting. Use their conversation to show the audience what kind of characters they are too. If you get stuck, don't worry. Write the story as a paragraph first. Then change it into dialogue.

Character Voice

How a character speaks dialogue tells audiences a lot about him or her.

Age, education, personality, and even where someone lives changes the way they speak.

Think about people you know. Your grandma doesn't talk like your cousin. Your best friend uses more **slang** than a teacher. The words you put into a character's mouth are his or her **voice**.

The photo you use to create your character can help you zero in on voice too. Try this. Make two columns on a piece of paper. Look at the photo, and think about how this queen might sound when she talks. In one column write a list of phrases that would sound natural for her to say. In the other, write things she would never say in a million years. You've just created her voice.

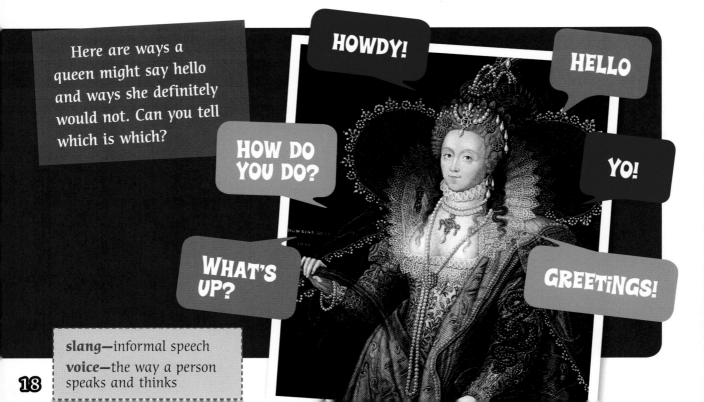

Here are ways a queen might say hello and ways she definitely would not. Can you tell which is which?

HOWDY!

HELLO

HOW DO YOU DO?

YO!

WHAT'S UP?

GREETINGS!

slang—informal speech
voice—the way a person speaks and thinks

write about it!

Imagine that a telephone rings. The person who called has the wrong number but doesn't believe it. Pretend the person in this picture answered the phone. Imagine her voice. How does she talk? Is she formal? Laid back? Does she use old-fashioned words? Write a skit about the phone call, giving each character a different voice.

Actions and Expressions

Movement is the name of the game in a drama. How your characters move on stage goes along with the dialogue to tell the story.

So how do you tell the actors what to do?

Playwrights include stage directions as part of the script. These directions go in parenthesis by the dialogue they go with.

When imagining how the characters will move, it helps to put yourself in their shoes. What would you do in the situation? A good photo can help you imagine movement.

Maybe your characters are rafting down a river. Imagine they lose their equipment when their raft tips over. How would you act if you thought someone tipped the raft on purpose? Would you wave your hands or stomp your feet? Would you yell or mutter? Weave those details into stage directions.

TOBY: (Points a finger at Amy, and shouts angrily) You flipped the raft on purpose!

AMY: (Hands on hips) Did not! (Pokes Toby in the chest) I saw you rocking back and forth.

write about It!

This guy is feeling some kind of emotion. Maybe he's angry, worried, tired, or bored. Decide what emotion this character is feeling. Then imagine that another character comes and sits beside him. Write dialogue between the two characters that explores how the man feels. Add stage directions that tell how the characters should move and act on stage.

Chapter 4

SCENE IT

Opening Scenes

A scene in a drama is like a chapter of a book.

Each scene shows a part of the drama that happens in a single setting. A good opening scene gets the audience interested in the story. An opening scene needs to introduce the setting, the main character, and the character's goal or problem.

Need help getting started? Let a photo become your idea factory. This photo might inspire an opening scene about characters sneaking onto a plane. Before you start to write, make a checklist and fill in the blanks.

Setting: **The airport at night.** The main characters: **Maya and Paulo**
The goal and action: **Getting to a baseball game by sneaking onto a plane.**

Now you're ready to write an opening scene that will hook your audience.

SCENE: (An airport at night.) Maya and Paulo tiptoe past a guard and hide behind a crate.

PAULO: (quietly) We're gonna get caught!

MAYA: (annoyed) Paulo, do you want to see the baseball game or not?

PAULO: (covers his head with his hands) Jail. We're going to jail.

MAYA: Shh! If we hide in this crate, we can fly for free. Hurry up. (Maya and Paulo climb inside the crate.)

write about It!

Let this photo inspire ideas for an opening scene. Who is the main character? What does the character want, and how will that happen? Where does the scene take place? Write an opening scene that answers those questions using dialogue. Use stage directions to create action on the stage.

middle scenes

Welcome to the **heart** of your **drama.**

The middle scenes are where the plot gets interesting. Here your character will face the challenges that stand in the way of the goal.

Problems are no fun in real life. But in a drama, complications keep the plot rolling. They pull the audience into the story and make them want to know what happens next. How do you get people's hearts pounding? Use a trick called rising action.

Rising action happens when your character faces a series of problems that continue to get tougher to solve. Each problem should lead to a new complication. When the character reaches the toughest challenge, that's the **climax** of the story.

Tap into photos for problem ideas, such as a flat tire. Then brainstorm ways the problem could lead to a bigger one.

Because the hero has a flat tire	→	the villain escapes.
Because the villain escapes	→	the hero follows and is captured in a trap.
Because the hero is trapped	→	he may be too late to save the world.

write about It!

Let this image get your mind inventing possible problems. Is the character lost or trapped? How can that problem create another? Create a chart showing how one problem leads to another and another and another. When you finish, use your chart to write two scenes featuring rising action.

climax—the most exciting part of a story

The End

Does the main character achieve the goal? The final scene of a drama tells the audience the answer. Maybe your story has a happy ending. Maybe it doesn't. How do you decide?

Use an image to think up several ways the action could end. In your brainstorming session, try to imagine at least three different ways to end a play. Challenge yourself to include unhappy endings and endings with a twist.

This picture might make you think of a drama about a big race. Here are some ideas about how it might end.

- The horse and rider lose the race but get an amazing opportunity to race next year.
- During the race, the horse gets spooked and runs the wrong way. The horse and rider don't finish the race.
- The horse and rider win, but the horse dies.

Once you have your list of endings, decide which idea inspires your imagination most. That's the idea to write your story around. A funny story will match up nicely with a happy ending. A serious story might end with a twist.

Write about It!

Imagine the story behind this picture. What does the character want? Does he get it? Make a list of at least three different endings for this situation. What kinds of twists can you dream up? Take your favorite idea, and write an out-of-this-world final scene.

A World of Inspiration

When you **look** at a photo, you open the **curtain** on your **imagination**.

One snapshot might drop you in the middle of a great setting. Another could spark an idea for a whole story.

A photo may stir up a unique character or inspire dialogue that makes a character real. Photos are amazing tools to help bring drama to life.

Photos are everywhere. Magazines, books, and newspapers are all good places to find them. Flip through family photos, old calendars, and greeting cards too. Look around. What stories are hiding in the photos around you?

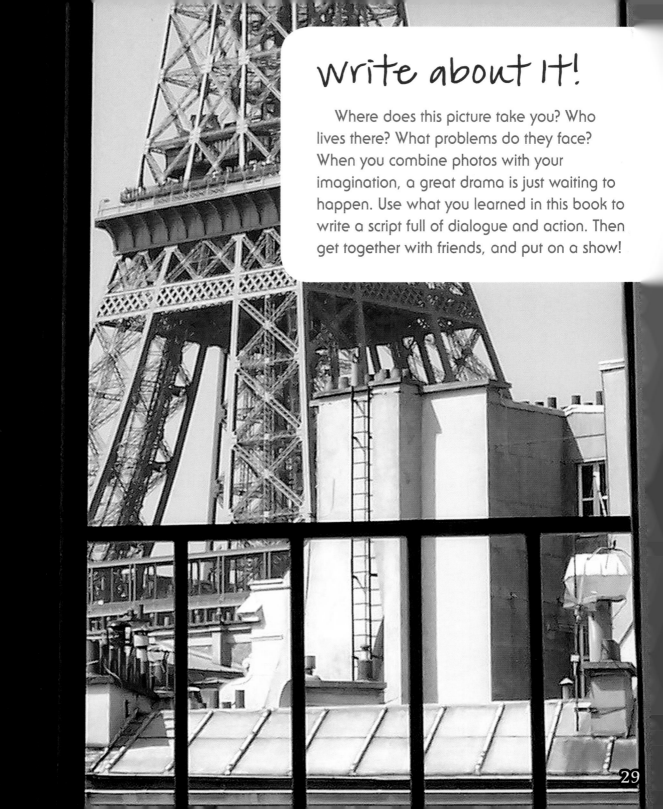

write about It!

Where does this picture take you? Who lives there? What problems do they face? When you combine photos with your imagination, a great drama is just waiting to happen. Use what you learned in this book to write a script full of dialogue and action. Then get together with friends, and put on a show!

GLOSSARY

backstory (BAK-stor-ee)—a story that tells what happened before the main story

climax (KLYE-maks)—the most exciting part of a story, usually happening near the end

medium (MEE-dee-uhm)—something that communicates messages; TV, movies, and the Internet are all mediums

monologue (MON-uh-log)—a long speech by one character in a drama

scene (SEEN)—a part of a story, play, or movie that shows what is happening in one place and time

setting (SET-ing)—the place where a drama takes place

skit (SKIT)—a short play that is often funny

slang (SLANG)—informal speech that is not considered standard

voice (VOISS)—the speech and thoughts of a character

READ MORE

Elish, Dan. *Plays.* The Craft of Writing. New York: Marshall Cavendish Benchmark, 2011.

Kenney, Karen Latchana. *Cool Scripts and Acting: How to Stage Your Very Own Show.* Cool Performances. Edina, Minn.: ABDO Pub. Company, 2010.

Miles, Liz. *Writing a Screenplay.* Culture in Action. Chicago: Raintree, 2010.

INTERNET SITES

FactHound offers a safe, fun way to find Internet sites related to this book. All of the sites on FactHound have been researched by our staff.

Here's all you do:

Visit *www.facthound.com*

Type in this code: 9781429661263

Check out projects, games and lots more at
www.capstonekids.com

INDEX

ABOUT THE AUTHOR

Barbara A. Tyler wrote her first drama when she was 9 years old. Since then, she's written and published stories, greeting cards, poems, crafts, and more. She enjoys helping young people find new ways to write and tell stories.